ParentsCAN

ParentsCAN
3299 Claremont Way, Ste.3
Napa, CA 94558

The Don't-give-up Kid

AND LEARNING DIFFERENCES

The Don't-give-up Kid

AND LEARNING DIFFERENCES

BY JEANNE GEHRET, M.A.
Illustrations and design by Sandra Ann DePauw

Verbal Images Press
Fairport, New York

The author wishes to thank the following people who served as consultants on this book:

Francis Bennett, Ph.D., Clinical Developmental Psychologist; **Roberta Beyer**, Assistant Superintendent of Schools, Penfield, New York; **Patricia Bourcy**, Training Specialist, City School District of Rochester; **Kathryn Cappella**, Association for the Learning Disabled of Genesee Valley; **Jayne Gifford**, Executive Director, Camp Fire, Rochester/Monroe County; **Bernie Kumetat, M.D.**, Child Psychiatrist; **Virginia McHugh**, Administrator, Montessori School of Rochester; **Daniel Nussbaum II, M.D.**, Genesee Developmental Center

ISBN 0-9625136-2-8 softcover
ISBN 0-9625136-3-6 hardcover
© 1990 Jeanne Gehret, M.A.
illustrations © 1990 Sandra Ann DePauw
second edition, second printing
Printed in Mexico

Publisher's Cataloging-in-Publication Data
Gehret, Jeanne.
   The don't-give-up kid and learning differences / by Jeanne Gehret ; illustrations and design by Sandra Ann DePauw.
   p. cm.
   Includes bibliographical references.
   SUMMARY: As Alex becomes aware of his different learning style, he realizes his hero Thomas Edison had similar problems. Together they try new solutions until they succeed at their dream to create things that no one ever thought of before.
   ISBN 0-9625136-2-8(pbk.)
   ISBN 0-9625136-3-6(hbk.)
   1. Learning ability--Juvenile fiction. 2. Learning--Methods--Juvenile fiction. I. DePauw, Sandra A. II. Title
   LB1134.G4 1990   808.89'9282   QBI91-1853

Verbal Images Press

19 Fox Hill Drive • Fairport, New York 14450
(716) 377-3807 • Fax (716) 377-5401

To my Don't-give-up Kid:
may all of your dreams come true

My name is Alex. But Mom calls me the Don't-give-up Kid because I keep finding new ways to ask the same question.

I want to be a famous inventor like Thomas Edison, the man who invented light bulbs. And I've been working on some inventions of my own.

Before I can become an inventor, though, Dad says I have to learn to read and behave in school. And when it comes to school, I stop being the Don't-give-up Kid. That's because school is where everything goes wrong.

And I mean *everything*.

Here's what happened on one of my worst days.

Before school Mrs. Potter, my teacher, asked me to help her unpack some new books. Holding them together was a giant rubber band — just what I needed for the chopper I was making. I took it to my desk.

Then I looked up. Mrs. Potter was standing by my desk, and the other kids were standing for Opening Exercises. She took my rubber band and said I could have it back at the end of the day.

After Opening Exercises, it started to rain outside. I wondered if I could invent a bubble big enough to keep me dry. I started to draw bubbles on my book.

"Alex, your turn to read," said Mrs. Potter. Everyone was watching me. I couldn't find the place for the longest time. Then she walked over to my desk and said, "Alex, put down your pencil and pay attention." She pointed to where I was supposed to read.

I stared at my book. Had I ever seen those letters before? The words seemed to jump around the page. Some looked backwards. Nobody made a sound while I tried to figure out what it said.

Then I began to read slowly so I could get every word right. "My hat is on pot of my head," I said. The boy behind me put his head down and started to laugh. Soon the whole class was laughing with him.

"On *top*, Alex," said Mrs. Potter. "Not *on pot.*"

I don't like to read, even at home. Dad said I just have to try harder. "Come on, Alex. I've read *Edison the Inventor* to you lots of times. Now let's read it together."

I asked him if we could play checkers instead.

One day Mom asked me if I'd like to have a friend over.

"How about that nice boy who sits next to you? What's his name?" she asked.

"Mark," I answered. But Mark wasn't nice. He made fun of me when I said "dead" instead of "bed." I felt like crawling under my desk so he couldn't look at me anymore.

"Well, how about Mark?" she asked.

"I don't think so," I replied, and turned away.

A few days after that, Mom took me to see Dr. Powell, who is a psychologist. He's not like my other doctor who gives me shots and checks my eyes. Instead, he asked me to tell him about the pictures in his book and connect the dots on his drawings.

Then he wanted to know about school. I told him how hard it is to read and stay out of trouble.

"I guess I'm just stupid," I said.

Later Mom sat on my bed to talk. "Alex," she said, "Dr. Powell told us why you're having trouble in school. You're very smart, but he said you learn in a different way from other children.

"When most people read, the letters stay in one place on the page, but for you they jump around.

"Most kids can pay attention when there are many things to look at. But you see everything at once. It's hard for you to concentrate."

She looked right into my eyes. "Would you like to do better in school?"

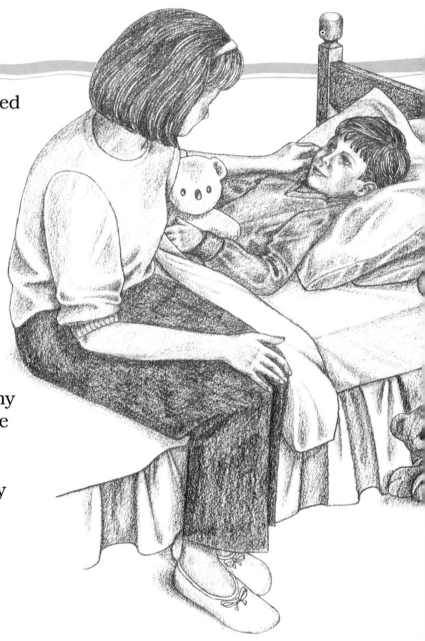

I stared at my favorite blanket. "No."

"Why not, Alex? I thought you were the Don't-give-up Kid." She winked at me, but her smile was sad.

"Because I can't!" I said, trying not to cry. "I try so hard, but I still can't read. And I'm always doing the wrong thing!"

"When you want something at home, Alex," Mom said, "you know how you keep trying one thing after another until I say yes?" I nodded. "Kids who learn differently need to try new ways to learn. I talked to the principal and they're going to let you work with Mrs. Baxter. She'll help you find your special way to learn."

And that's when things began to get better.

Mrs. Baxter's room is different. It's smaller and quieter than my regular class, so I can concentrate better. Best of all, Mrs. Baxter spends a lot of time with me. She makes me feel really special.

At first, I was afraid she'd give me long books that I couldn't read. And that she'd think I was stupid. But she didn't.

Instead, Mrs. Baxter gave me a card with just one word on it: run. Then another card: sun. With only one word on each card, I could put the letters back together pretty quickly if they jumped around.

Another card: bun. Or was it gun?

She waited. I didn't want to make a mistake, so I didn't answer.

Then she told me a story about Thomas Edison, the inventor. One of his inventions took 10,000 tries before it would work.

One day he was asked, "How does it feel to have failed 10,000 times?"

"I didn't fail 10,000 times," Mr. Edison answered. "I succeeded at finding 10,000 ways that don't work." After many more tries, his invention was a big success.

If I want to be like Mr. Edison, I have to keep trying too.

"Come on, Alex, don't give up," I said to myself, and concentrated hard on the word in front of me.

"B-un," I read slowly.

Mrs. Baxter nodded and gave me another card to read. I felt really good.

Since then, I've done lots of reading with her. She makes it fun. If I finish my work ahead of time, she lets me play checkers with the other kids.

All the kids who work with Mrs. Baxter have a learning difference. That means some kinds of learning are hard for us. She says we're not stupid; we just need to find our own ways to learn.

Shelly has trouble remembering what she *hears*. She never used to follow directions. Now she can, because Mrs. Baxter writes things down for her.

Jonathan has trouble writing, even though he can read. So now when he takes a test, he tells the teacher the answers and she writes them for him. Otherwise he'd never finish writing.

It's hard for Michael to say what he's thinking, and people used to call him stupid. But he can *write* just fine — much better than I can.

My parents told me that nobody knows how kids gets learning differences. You can't catch them, like a cold. Some people think you're born with them.

Sometimes I work with Shelly and Michael and Jonathan. They don't laugh when I make mistakes. Michael even came to my birthday party.

Some kids need special ways to learn, just like other kids need help for other things.

My sister Kate is five and she still needs training wheels on her bike. Otherwise she loses her balance and falls off.

You should see her knees!

My neighbor Kerri has to wear braces. Her teeth are too big for her mouth.

I think my cousin Sarah has the worst problem of all, though — she has to get shots every month or she sneezes all the time.

Even a Don't-give-up Kid wants to quit when the going gets tough. But if something's important to you, I guess you just have to keep working at it till you get it right.

Mrs. Baxter won't let me give up on reading. Thanks to her, I can read better now.

Now I can read cereal boxes. And street signs as we drive to the store.

And every night Dad reads to me from the book about Thomas Edison. Did you know that Mr. Edison had trouble writing? Maybe he had a learning difference, too.

Dad said many famous people have learning differences. Some have made famous statues and paintings. One was governor of New York. Others have become singers and actors. And another won the Olympics!

These people had trouble learning, but they kept trying. And their learning problems didn't keep them from doing other things very well.

I can swim really fast. I can do my cousin's math, even though he's two years older than I am. And I can make things that no one ever thought of before. So I'm not going to let my problems with reading make me feel bad about myself anymore.

Someday I'll read
that Thomas Edison book
all by myself. But first I
want to try out my latest
invention: a propeller,
made with giant rubber
bands, to wear on my back
and make me fly.

And if that doesn't work, I'll just strap on some helium balloons.

PARENT RESOURCE GUIDE

Our role as parents of youngsters who learn differently

In 1982, I gave birth to an exceptional child. Unfortunately, my husband and I didn't know it. Thus our early years of parenting were like driving a road rally without a map—most of our trials resulted in errors. Then in 1988 we found the answer to Danny's bewildering and frustrating behaviors: he was diagnosed with learning differences (LD) and attention deficit disorder.

Danny's diagnosis unleashed in us a host of conflicting emotions: relief that his problem was neurological rather than something we'd caused through "bad parenting;" guilt over episodes when we'd punished him for something he couldn't help doing; fear for the future; and hopelessness about our ability to follow all the prescriptions for behavioral and educational modifications.

Although we reached out for every kind of help available, we resented our family's need for therapists and specialized education plans. Why did everything have to be such a struggle? Why couldn't we just be like other families?

Here are some steps we've taken to enjoy life with our exceptional son, who is assuming his birthright as a happy, intelligent, talented young man. Try these simple changes now to improve your family life:

1) See that your child gets an appropriate education. Although this may take lots of effort, it's worth it. As your youngster's academic skills increase, so will self-esteem and independence. School frustration will decrease, and your child will come home happier at the end of each day.

2) Remind yourself that learning differences affect home life as much as school performance. Because she has LD, your youngster may be likely to forget things she's already learned; spill frequently; have difficulty finding the right words to say; have trouble getting organized, and miss the punch line of jokes. She may need extra help and encouragement to learn simple home and social routines.

3) Explain to your child the difference between mental retardation and learning differences.

People with mental retardation have below-average intelligence and there are some things they'll never be able to learn. LD students have average intelligence or higher, and are able to learn most things if they receive the appropriate instruction.

4)   Accept the child you have rather than lamenting the one you don't have. This will open your eyes to the real progress he makes in areas that may surprise you.

5)   Help your youngster overcome disorganization and dependence at home by choosing tasks you know she can do, by coaching her methodically in those jobs, and by increasing her responsibility when you see that she has mastered simple steps.

6)   Point out successful adults who have had LD: Bruce Jenner, champion in the 1976 summer Olympics; Cher, the famous singer; Thomas Edison; Albert Einstein, winner of the 1921 Nobel Prize for Physics; Leonardo DaVinci, painter of the Mona Lisa; Auguste Rodin, sculptor and artist; General George Patton; Nelson Rockefeller, vice president of the United States. Add to this list to inspire your child.

Many successful adults with learning differences say that during their youth they received large doses of support from a caring adult. We parents can influence our LD children by giving them an honest appraisal of their weaknesses and showing them how to compensate. And we can give them a mile-long list of ways to apply their strengths.

Exceptional children need exceptional parents. Welcome to the ranks.

Jeanne Gehret, 1991

PARENT RESOURCE GUIDE

A list of the specific learning differences described in
The Don't-give-up Kid:
(* indicates a character from this book)

- **auditory processing** - difficulty understanding what one hears, or problems distinguishing between different sounds. Shelly* has a problem with auditory processing.
- **dyslexia** - problems remembering and recognizing written letters, numbers, and words; may result in backwards reading or poor handwriting. Alex* has dyslexia.
- **dysgraphia** - difficulty expressing thoughts through writing. Jonathan* has dysgraphia.
- **expressive language disability** - difficulty expressing oneself through speech. Michael* has an expressive language disability.

People with learning disabilities may also have problems with:

- **attention** - inability to focus on relevant information, screen out distractions, or stay on task. Alex* has attention problems because of his learning disabilities. Some children with Attention Deficit Disorder may have attention problems *without* learning disabilities.
- **memory** - difficulties remembering things that happened a short or long time ago.
- **sequencing** - knowing and carrying through procedures in a particular order.
- **visual perception** - difficulty distinguishing one visual element from another.

For more information, contact:

- Your local school district's Committee on Special Education (also called Child Study Team)
- Learning Disabilities Association of America, 4156 Library Road, Pittsburgh, PA 15234**
- Orton Dyslexia Society, 724 York Road, Baltimore, MD 21204**

**Look for state and local chapters of these organizations

Selected resources on learning differences and attention problems

For students:

- Margaret Cousins, *The Story of Thomas Alva Edison.* Random House. 10-14 yrs.
- Gary Fisher, Ph.D. and Rhoda Cummings, ED.D., *The Survival Guide for Kids with LD.* Free Spirit Publishing, Inc., 400 First Avenue NO., Suite 616, Minneapolis, MN 55401. 10 yrs & up.
- Jeanne Gehret, M.A., *Eagle Eyes: A Child's Guide to Paying Attention.* Verbal Images Press, 19 Fox Hill Drive, Fairport, NY 14450. 6 to 10 yrs.
- Caroline Janover, *Josh: A Boy with Dyslexia.* Waterfront Books, Burlington, VT 05401. 10-14 yrs.

For adults:

- Nathan H. Azrin and Victoria A. Besalel, *Parents Guide to Bedwetting Control: A Step-by-Step Method.* Pocket Books.
- Melody Beattie, *Codependent No More: How to Stop Controlling Others and Start Caring for Yourself.* Harper and Row.
- Ronald J. Friedman and Guy T. Doyal, *Attention Deficit Disorder and Hyperactivity.* Pro-Ed, 8700 Shoal Creek Boulevard, Austin, TX 78758.
- Michael Gordon, Ph.D., *ADHD/Hyperactivity: A Consumer's Guide For Parents & Teachers.* GSI Publications, PO Box 746, DeWitt, NY 13214.
- Barbara Ingersoll, *Your Hyperactive Child: A Parents Guide to Coping with ADD.* Doubleday.
- Richard Lavoie, "How Difficult Can This Be?" (video to simulate the feelings of a child with LD) PBS Video, 1320 Braddock Place, Alexandria, VA 22314.
- Betty Osman, *No One to Play With: The Social Side of Learning Disabilities.* Academic Therapy Publications.
- Harvey C. Parker, *The ADD Hyperactivity Workbook for Parents, Teachers, and Kids.* Impact Publications, 300 NW 70th Ave., Plantation, FL 33317.
- Suzanne Stevens, *Helping the LD Student with Homework.* LDTV, 134 Shady Boulevard, Winston-Salem, NC, 27101.
- Sally L. Smith, *No Easy Answers: The Learning Disabled Child at Home and at School.* Bantam Books.
- John Taylor, *Helping Your Hyperactive Child.* SUN Books, 5406 Battlecreek Road SE, Salem, OR 97306.

Works by Jeanne Gehret

Eagle Eyes: A Child's Guide to Paying Attention, 1991, second edition. Ages 6 to 10. 40-page picture book with newly-revised parent resource guide. Hardcover or paperback.

The Don't-give-up Kid and Learning Differences, 1990, second edition. Ages 6 to 10. 40-page picture book with newly-revised parent resource guide. Hardcover or paperback.

Watch for new titles in 1992 and beyond.

For a book brochure with complete ordering information, check below.

Looking for a speaker? Check below to receive a brochure entitled "Unforgettable Author Visits". Jeanne Gehret, guest of dozens of radio and TV shows, has brought her message of hope and practical advice to students, teachers, librarians, and parents nationwide.

Please send me more information:

_____ Book brochure on *Eagle Eyes* and *The Don't-give-up Kid*
_____ Brochure on new books
_____ Quantity discounts
_____ Author visit brochure

Name _____

Street _____

City, state, zip _____

Verbal Images Press

19 Fox Hill Drive • Fairport, New York 14450
(716) 377-3807 • Fax (716) 377-5401